GREAT GRAPH ART
Around the Year

By Deborah Schecter

SCHOLASTIC
PROFESSIONAL BOOKS

New York ☆ Toronto ☆ London ☆ Auckland ☆ Sydney
Mexico City ☆ New Delhi ☆ Hong Kong ☆ Buenos Aires

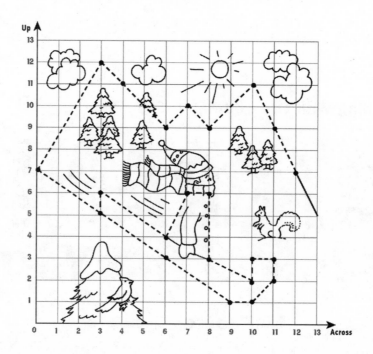

Cover and interior art by Kate Flanagan
Cover design by Maria Lilja
Interior design by Pamela Simmons

ISBN: 0-439-45338-0
Copyright © 2003 by Deborah Schecter.
Published by Scholastic Inc.
All rights reserved.
Printed in the U.S.A.
2 3 4 5 6 7 8 9 10   40   09 08 07 06 05 04 03

Contents

Sensational Spring & Summer

Coordinate Graphing With Multiplication and Division

About This Book

Welcome to *Great Graph Art Around the Year!* In the reproducible activities that follow, your students will get lots of practice sharpening math skills and plotting ordered pairs on a graph. In the process, they'll have lots of fun creating picture surprises that celebrate holiday and seasonal occasions around the year including Thanksgiving, winter holidays, Valentine's Day, Cinco de Mayo, and more.

How to Use This Book

● In the first chapter, Fall Fun, students practice the basics of coordinate graphing. First, they read a chart containing sets of number (ordered) pairs. Next, they find points on a graph based on each ordered pair. Then, using a straightedge, they connect the points in the order they plotted them to see a picture surprise emerge! For example, in Harvest Time, on page 10, have students find the point on the graph that corresponds with the ordered pair (16, 44). Then they plot the point for the second ordered pair (20, 40) and use a straightedge to connect the two points. They continue in this matter to create a silly scarecrow.

● In Wonderful Winter and Sensational Spring & Summer, students first solve addition, subtraction, multiplication, and division problems to determine the ordered pairs. (The skill focus of each activity appears at the top of each page.) Then they plot each pair, in order, on a graph and use a straightedge to connect the points.

Tips

● To help students keep their place on the worksheet page as they plot each set of points, they may find it helpful to mask the rest of the page with a sheet of paper.

● To make the graph art pictures show up better on the grids, students can use colored pencils to plot and connect the points.

● In some of the activities, students will plot the same point twice.

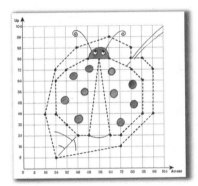

● Three activities include a Here's More! section (Lucky Charm, page 38; Creepy Crawly, page 44; and April Showers, page 50). Invite students to solve the additional problems and then plot the answers on their graph to add to their picture.

Taking It Further

After students have graphed the pictures, invite them to color and add details to their graph art creations using crayons, markers, or colored pencils. Then create a Graph Art Gallery bulletin board in your classroom. Students will love seeing their artwork displayed.

To extend students' graph art experience, invite them to come up with their own sets of math problems and accompanying graph pictures for classmates to solve and create!

Name _____

So Long, Summer!

1. Find each number pair on the graph. Make a dot for each. The first one has been done for you.

2. Connect the dots in the order that you make them.

3. What picture did you make?

	Across	Up			Across	Up
1.	1	1	8.		11	7
2.	1	7	9.		11	1
3.	4	8	10.		8	1
4.	4	10	11.		8	6
5.	6	11	12.		4	6
6.	8	10	13.		4	1
7.	8	8	14.		1	1

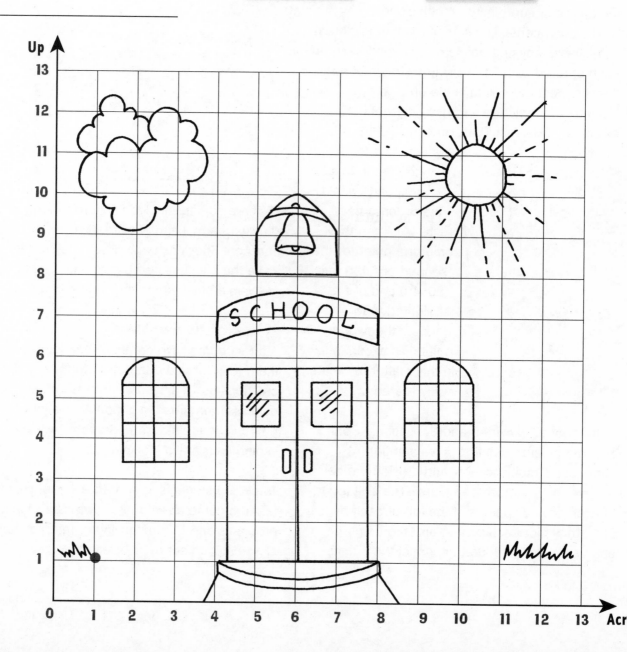

Name _____

Bag for Books

1. Find each number pair on the graph. Make a dot for each. The first one has been done for you.

	Across	Up
1.	3	10
2.	3	6
3.	6	6
4.	9	6
5.	9	10

	Across	Up
6.	10	2
7.	6	2
8.	2	2
9.	3	10
10.	9	10

2. Connect the dots in the order that you make them.

3. What picture did you make?

_____

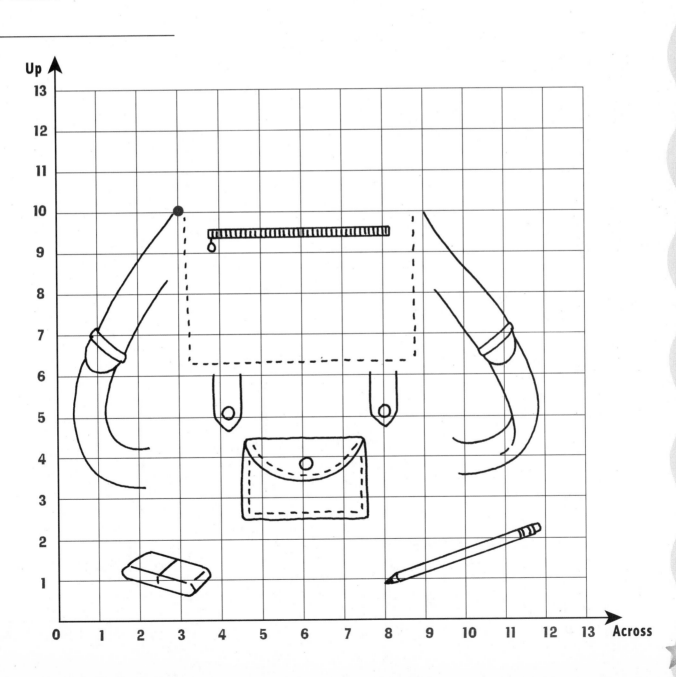

Coordinate Graphing
Fun in the Orchard

1. Find each number pair on the graph. Make a dot for each. The first one has been done for you.

2. Connect the dots in the order that you make them.

3. What picture did you make?

_____

	Across	Up			Across	Up
1.	3	1		**9.**	9	12
2.	5	2		**10.**	11	11
3.	5	5		**11.**	12	9
4.	3	5		**12.**	12	7
5.	1	7		**13.**	10	5
6.	1	9		**14.**	8	5
7.	2	11		**15.**	8	2
8.	4	12		**16.**	9	1

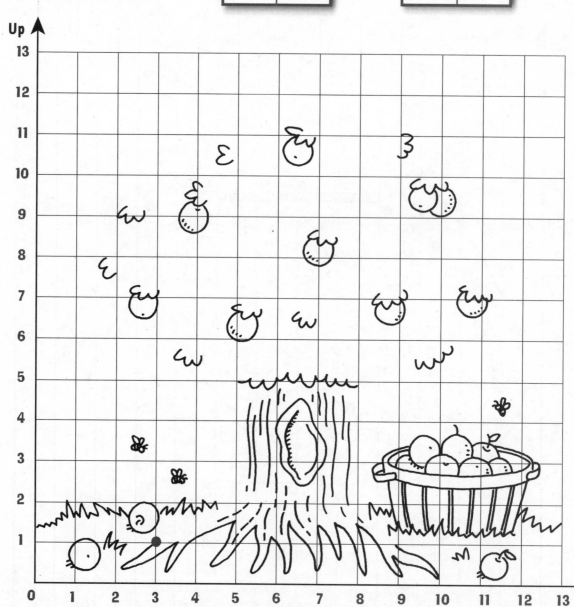

Trick-or-Treat!

1. Find each number pair on the graph. Make a dot for each. The first one has been done for you.

2. Connect the dots in the order that you make them.

3. What picture did you make?

_____

	Across	Up
1.	12	22
2.	14	20
3.	14	18
4.	16	18
5.	20	16
6.	22	14

	Across	Up
7.	22	8
8.	20	4
9.	16	2
10.	10	2
11.	6	4
12.	4	8

	Across	Up
13.	4	14
14.	6	16
15.	10	18
16.	12	18
17.	12	20
18.	10	22
19.	12	22

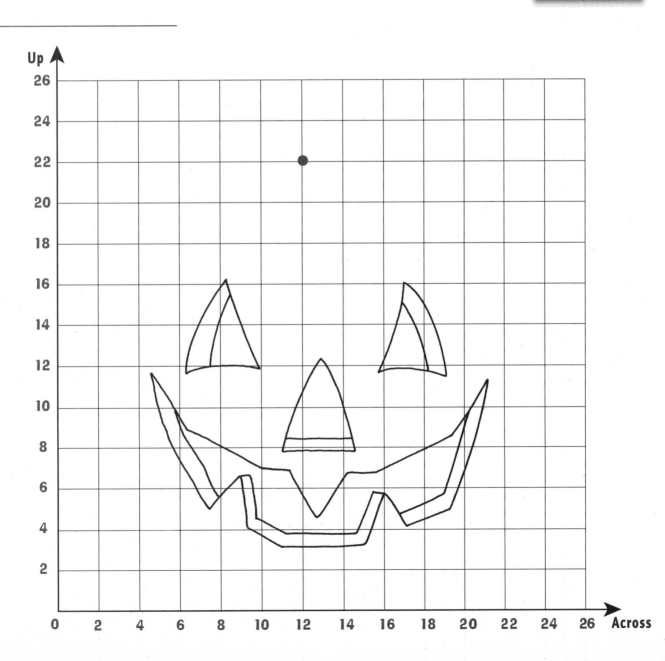

Coordinate Graphing

Harvest Time

Name _____

1. Find each number pair on the graph. Make a dot for each. The first one has been done for you.

2. Connect the dots in the order that you make them.

3. What picture did you make?

_____

	Across	Up
1.	16	44
2.	20	44
3.	20	40
4.	24	36
5.	8	36
6.	8	32
7.	16	32
8.	16	20

	Across	Up
9.	12	4
10.	20	4
11.	20	8
12.	24	20
13.	28	8
14.	28	4
15.	36	4
16.	32	20

	Across	Up
17.	32	32
18.	40	32
19.	40	36
20.	24	36
21.	28	40
22.	28	44
23.	32	44

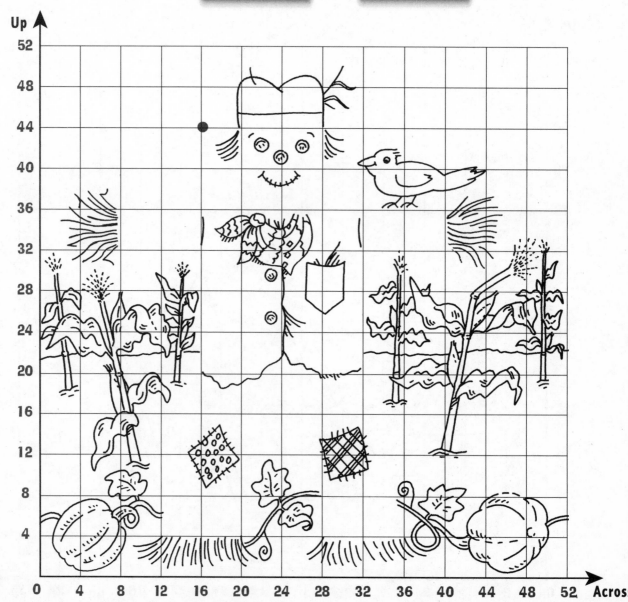

Great Graph Art Around the Year Scholastic Professional Books

Name _____

All Aboard!

1. Find each number pair on the graph. Make a dot for each. The first one has been done for you.

2. Connect the dots in the order that you make them.

3. What picture did you make?

_____

	Across	Up
1.	18	30
2.	6	30
3.	6	18
4.	18	12
5.	18	6
6.	54	6
7.	66	18
8.	66	30

	Across	Up
9.	54	30
10.	48	24
11.	30	24
12.	24	30
13.	18	30
14.	18	36
15.	30	36
16.	36	42

	Across	Up
17.	36	48
18.	30	72
19.	0	66
20.	6	54
21.	6	42
22.	0	36
23.	18	36

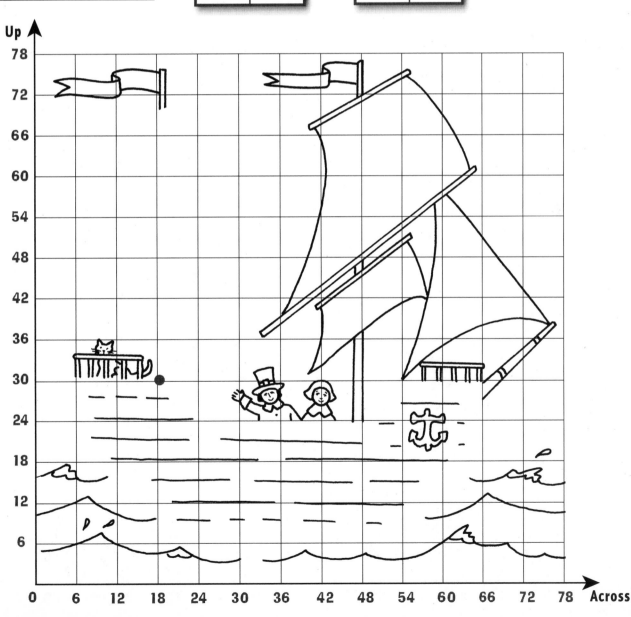

Name _____

Gobble! Gobble!

1. Find each number pair on the graph. Make a dot for each. The first one has been done for you.

2. Connect the dots in the order that you make them.

3. What picture did you make?

_____

	Across	Up
1.	50	25
2.	60	40
3.	50	30
4.	60	50
5.	45	35
6.	55	55
7.	45	40
8.	45	60

	Across	Up
9.	40	40
10.	35	55
11.	35	40
12.	30	50
13.	35	35
14.	20	30
15.	20	40
16.	15	45

	Across	Up
17.	10	45
18.	5	40
19.	5	30
20.	10	35
21.	15	35
22.	15	30

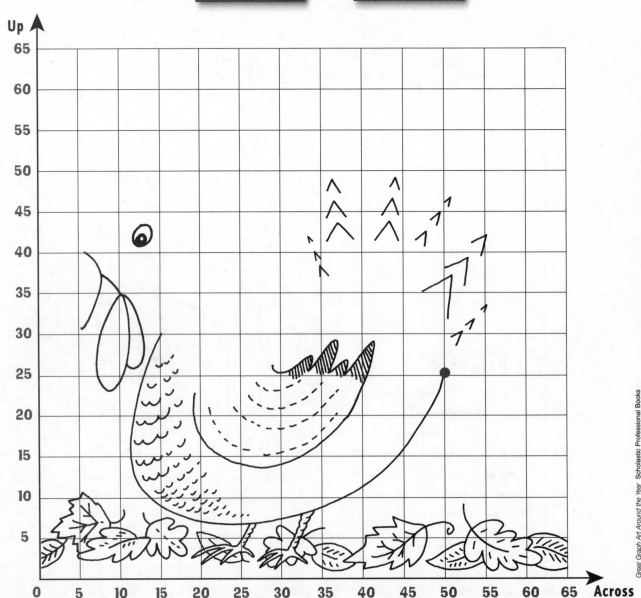

Holiday Dessert

1. Find each number pair on the graph. Make a dot for each. The first one has been done for you.

2. Connect the dots in the order that you make them.

3. What picture did you make?

_____

	Across	Up
1.	7	35
2.	21	21
3.	70	21
4.	84	35
5.	63	49
6.	28	49

	Across	Up
7.	7	35
8.	21	28
9.	49	28
10.	42	35
11.	35	35
12.	42	42

	Across	Up
13.	42	49
14.	49	42
15.	56	42
16.	49	35
17.	49	28
18.	70	28
19.	84	35

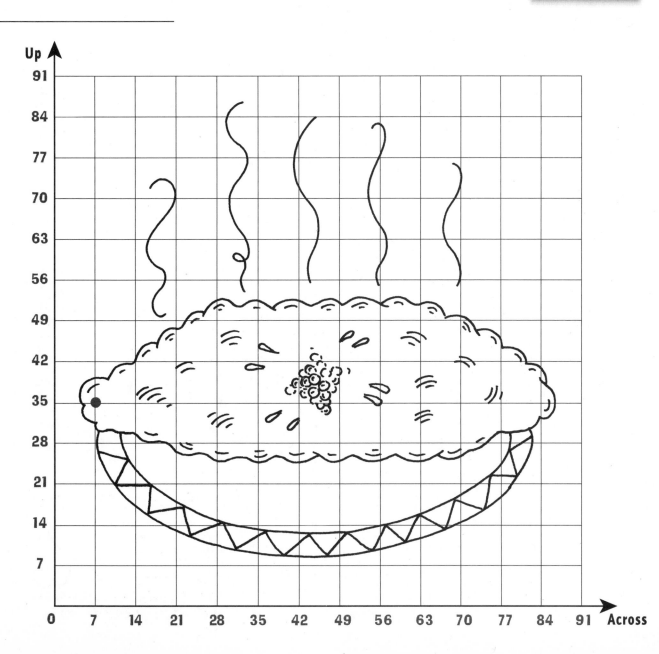

Name _____

Sweet Treat

1. Solve each problem. Example problems have been done for you.

2. Find each number pair on the graph on page 15.

3. Make a dot for each pair. Connect the dots in the order that you make them.

	Across			Up		
1.	4 + 8 = __12__			2 + 12 = __14__		(Example)
2.	1 + 3 = _____			3 + 3 = _____		
3.	2 + 2 = _____			0 + 4 = _____		
4.	2 + 10 = _____			7 + 5 = _____		
5.	6 + 6 = _____			2 + 0 = _____		
6.	8 + 6 = _____			1 + 1 = _____		
7.	11 + 3 = _____			9 + 5 = _____		
8.	19 + 1 = _____			13 + 7 = _____		
9.	11 + 11 = _____			3 + 17 = _____		
10.	17 + 5 = _____			9 + 9 = _____		
11.	15 + 5 = _____			5 + 13 = _____		
12.	11 + 9 = _____			7 + 9 = _____		
13.	19 + 3 = _____			4 + 12 = _____		
14.	12 + 12 = _____			7 + 11 = _____		
15.	1 + 23 = _____			12 + 8 = _____		
16.	16 + 6 = _____			13 + 9 = _____		
17.	2 + 18 = _____			7 + 15 = _____		
18.	2 + 12 = _____			5 + 11 = _____		
19.	5 + 9 = _____			4 + 18 = _____		
20.	3 + 9 = _____			19 + 5 = _____		
21.	0 + 10 = _____			16 + 8 = _____		
22.	5 + 3 = _____			9 + 13 = _____		
23.	6 + 2 = _____			3 + 15 = _____		
24.	9 + 1 = _____			6 + 12 = _____		
25.	4 + 6 = _____			14 + 8 = _____		
26.	11 + 1 = _____			10 + 12 = _____		
27.	4 + 8 = _____			7 + 7 = _____		

Great Graph Art Around the Year Scholastic Professional Books

Sweet Treat

1. Make a dot on the graph for each number pair on page 14.
The first one has been done for you.

2. Connect the points in the order that you make them.

3. What picture did you make?_____

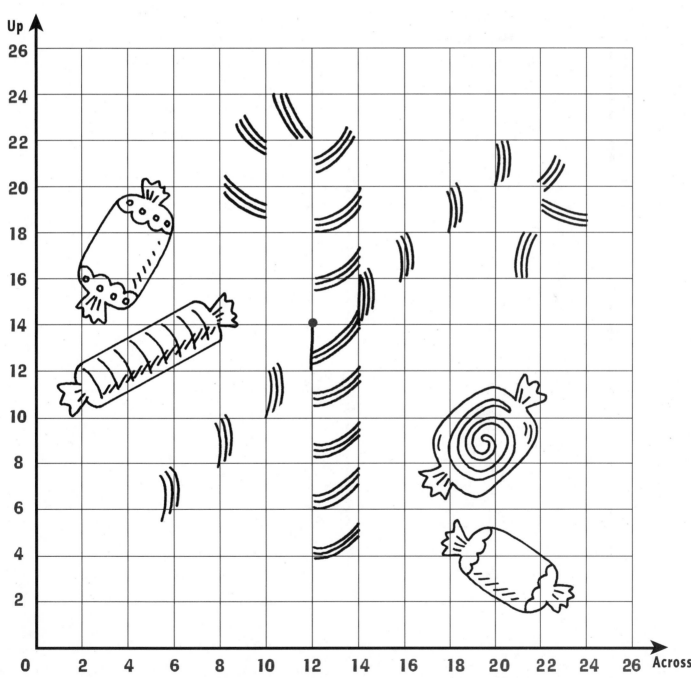

Name _____

Hanukkah Fun

1. Solve each problem. Example problems have been done for you.

2. Find each number pair on the graph on page 17. Make a dot for each pair.

3. Connect the dots in the order that you make them.

	Across	Up
1.	20 + 50 = __70__	42 + 21 = __63__ (Example)
2.	33 + 16 = _____	50 + 13 = _____
3.	17 + 32 = _____	54 + 23 = _____
4.	31 + 18 = _____	23 + 61 = _____
5.	11 + 31 = _____	52 + 32 = _____
6.	21 + 21 = _____	35 + 42 = _____
7.	40 + 2 = _____	41 + 22 = _____
8.	11 + 17 = _____	63 + 0 = _____
9.	0 + 21 = _____	33 + 23 = _____
10.	11 + 10 = _____	12 + 16 = _____
11.	31 + 11 = _____	3 + 4 = _____
12.	61 + 2 = _____	10 + 11 = _____
13.	40 + 30 = _____	14 + 14 = _____
14.	60 + 10 = _____	32 + 31 = _____
15.	12 + 51 = _____	13 + 43 = _____
16.	20 + 1 = _____	24 + 32 = _____

Great Graph Art Around the Year Scholastic Professional Books

Name ____________________

Hanukkah Fun

1. Make a dot on the graph for each number pair on page 16. The first one has been done for you.

2. Connect the points in the order that you make them.

3. What picture did you make?____________________

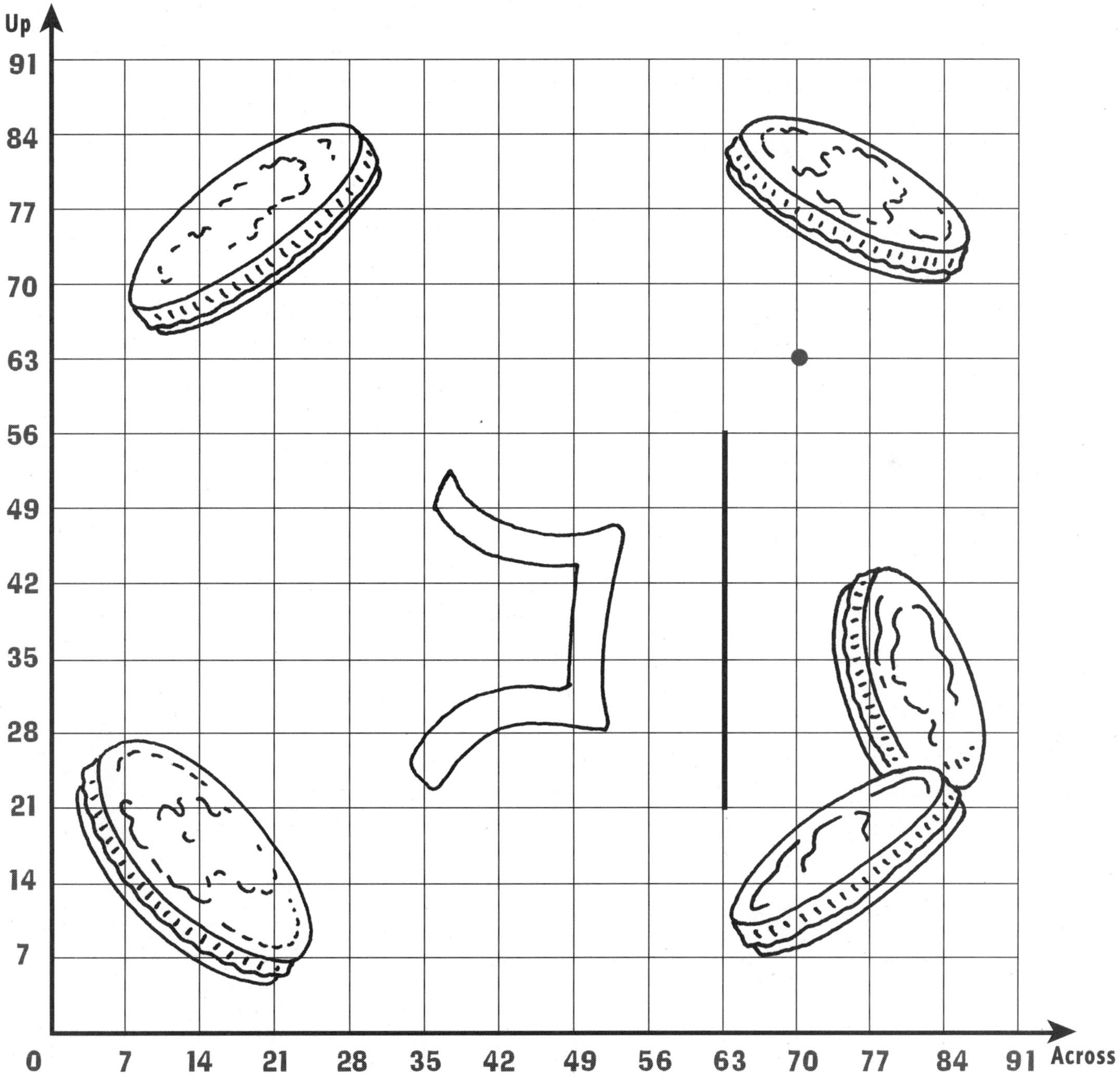
Up
91
84
77
70
63
56
49
42
35
28
21
14
7
0
7
14
21
28
35
42
49
56
63
70
77
84
91
Across

Name _____

Kwanzaa Time

1. Solve each problem. Example problems have been done for you.

2. Find each number pair on the graph on page 19.

3. Make a dot for each pair. Connect the dots in the order that you make them.

	Across		Up	
1.	49 + 8 = __57__		17 + 25 = __42__	(Example)
2.	35 + 16 = _____		36 + 9 = _____	
3.	14 + 19 = _____		37 + 8 = _____	
4.	18 + 9 = _____		35 + 7 = _____	
5.	29 + 28 = _____		14 + 28 = _____	
6.	18 + 39 = _____		11 + 28 = _____	
7.	8 + 19 = _____		23 + 16 = _____	
8.	17 + 16 = _____		9 + 27 = _____	
9.	18 + 33 = _____		17 + 19 = _____	
10.	39 + 18 = _____		4 + 29 = _____	
11.	28 + 23 = _____		8 + 19 = _____	
12.	39 + 15 = _____		19 + 14 = _____	
13.	15 + 24 = _____		18 + 12 = _____	
14.	8 + 19 = _____		18 + 18 = _____	
15.	19 + 5 = _____		23 + 16 = _____	
16.	0 + 0 = _____		19 + 20 = _____	
17.	0 + 0 = _____		37 + 5 = _____	
18.	9 + 15 = _____		23 + 19 = _____	
19.	8 + 19 = _____		38 + 7 = _____	
20.	27 + 27 = _____		26 + 25 = _____	
21.	27 + 24 = _____		37 + 17 = _____	
22.	48 + 9 = _____		32 + 19 = _____	
23.	6 + 45 = _____		29 + 16 = _____	

Great Graph Art Around the Year Scholastic Professional Books

Kwanzaa Time

1. Make a dot on the graph for each number pair on page 18.
   The first one has been done for you.

2. Connect the points in the order that you make them.

3. What picture did you make?_____

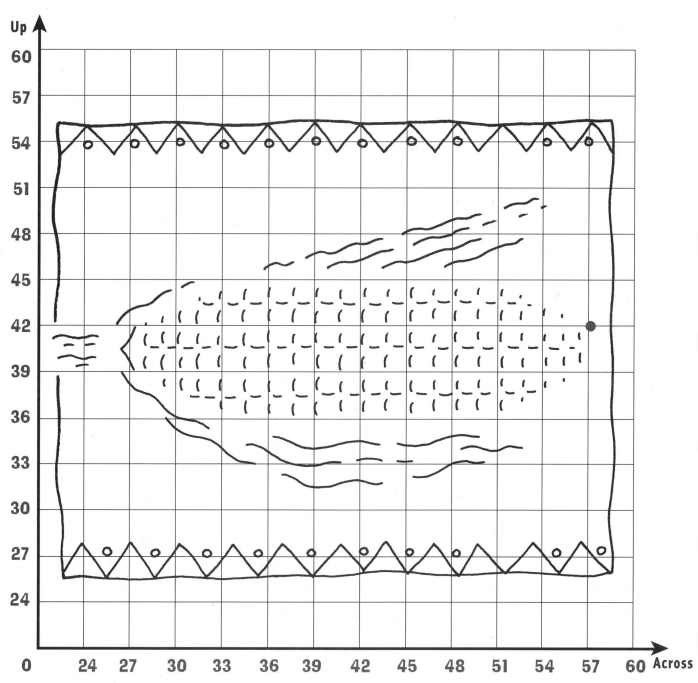

Name _____

Warm and Cozy

1. Solve each problem. Example problems have been done for you.

2. Find each number pair on the graph on page 21.

3. Make a dot for each pair. Connect the dots in the order that you make them.

	Across	Up
1.	30 – 28 = __2__	30 – 10 = __20__ (Example)
2.	17 – 15 = _____	20 – 18 = _____
3.	30 – 26 = _____	15 – 13 = _____
4.	19 – 15 = _____	30 – 14 = _____
5.	30 – 22 = _____	23 – 7 = _____
6.	26 – 18 = _____	29 – 15 = _____
7.	25 – 19 = _____	21 – 7 = _____
8.	19 – 13 = _____	24 – 12 = _____
9.	29 – 19 = _____	17 – 5 = _____
10.	30 – 20 = _____	21 – 5 = _____
11.	30 – 16 = _____	25 – 9 = _____
12.	26 – 12 = _____	20 – 6 = _____
13.	27 – 15 = _____	19 – 5 = _____
14.	19 – 7 = _____	25 – 13 = _____
15.	29 – 13 = _____	30 – 18 = _____
16.	27 – 11 = _____	18 – 2 = _____
17.	23 – 3 = _____	22 – 6 = _____
18.	29 – 9 = _____	23 – 9 = _____
19.	22 – 4 = _____	17 – 3 = _____
20.	26 – 8 = _____	29 – 17 = _____
21.	29 – 7 = _____	20 – 8 = _____
22.	27 – 5 = _____	20 – 4 = _____
23.	29 – 5 = _____	28 – 12 = _____
24.	25 – 1 = _____	18 – 16 = _____
25.	29 – 3 = _____	27 – 25 = _____
26.	26 – 0 = _____	28 – 8 = _____
27.	17 – 15 = _____	20 – 0 = _____

Great Graph Art Around the Year Scholastic Professional Books

Warm and Cozy

Name _____

1. Make a dot on the graph for each number pair on page 19.
   The first one has been done for you.

2. Connect the points in the order that you make them.

3. What picture did you make? _____

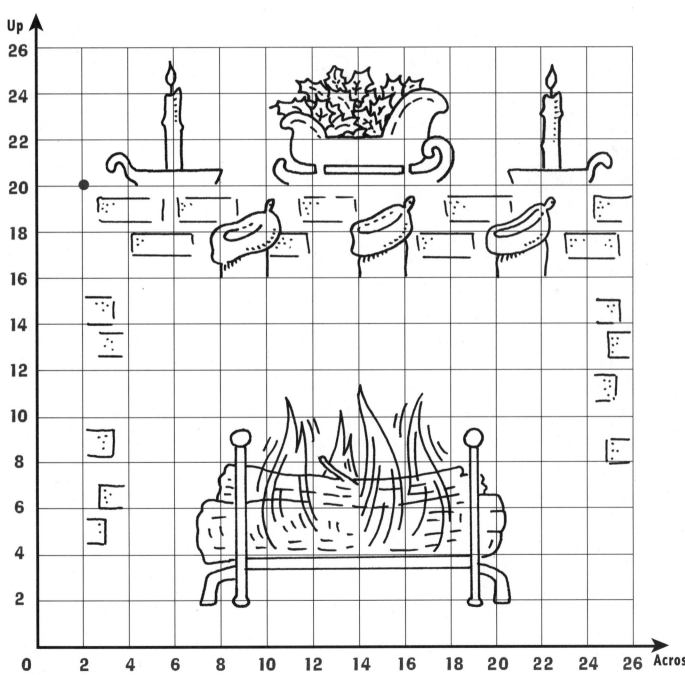

Name _____

Happy New Year!

1. Solve each problem. Example problems have been done for you.

2. Find each number pair on the graph on page 23.

3. Make a dot for each pair. Connect the dots in the order that you make them.

	Across	Up
1.	45 – 30 = __15__	49 – 19 = __30__ (Example)
2.	39 – 14 = _____	47 – 12 = _____
3.	77 – 42 = _____	56 – 16 = _____
4.	95 – 50 = _____	49 – 14 = _____
5.	68 – 13 = _____	50 – 10 = _____
6.	60 – 10 = _____	88 – 43 = _____
7.	72 – 32 = _____	86 – 36 = _____
8.	38 – 13 = _____	66 – 11 = _____
9.	48 – 13 = _____	98 – 43 = _____
10.	83 – 33 = _____	75 – 25 = _____
11.	79 – 19 = _____	68 – 23 = _____
12.	82 – 22 = _____	66 – 31 = _____
13.	97 – 42 = _____	48 – 23 = _____
14.	59 – 14 = _____	64 – 44 = _____
15.	87 – 52 = _____	47 – 22 = _____
16.	75 – 45 = _____	33 – 13 = _____
17.	67 – 42 = _____	96 – 81 = _____
18.	28 – 13 = _____	46 – 16 = _____

Great Graph Art Around the Year Scholastic Professional Books

Name _____

Happy New Year!

1. Make a dot on the graph for each number pair on page 22.
The first one has been done for you.

2. Connect the points in the order that you make them.

3. What picture did you make? _____

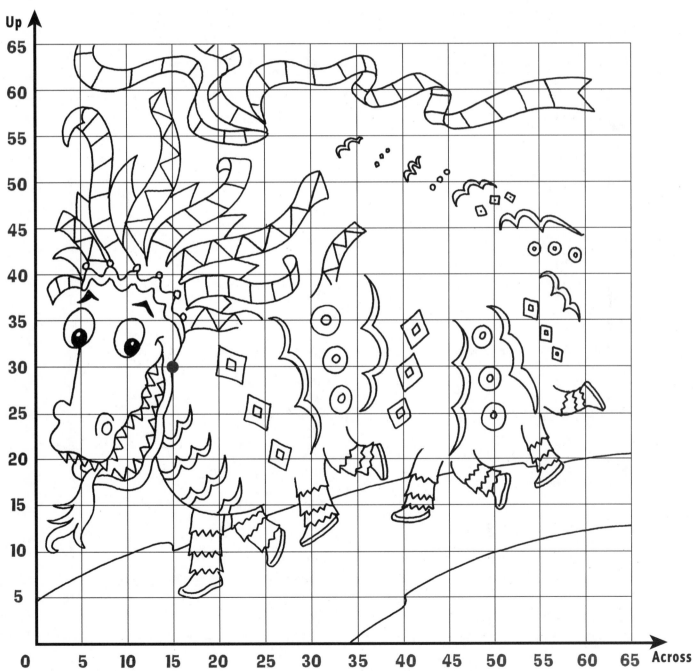

Name _____

The Shadow Knows

1. Solve each problem. Example problems have been done for you.

2. Find each number pair on the graph on page 25.

3. Make a dot for each pair. Connect the dots in the order that you make them.

	Across	Up
1.	74 – 18 = __56__	31 – 17 = __14__ (Example)
2.	79 – 9 = _____	55 – 48 = _____
3.	94 – 17 = _____	52 – 38 = _____
4.	90 – 13 = _____	40 – 19 = _____
5.	86 – 16 = _____	43 – 15 = _____
6.	72 – 16 = _____	51 – 16 = _____
7.	91 – 28 = _____	61 – 19 = _____
8.	80 – 17 = _____	75 – 19 = _____
9.	74 – 18 = _____	81 – 18 = _____
10.	65 – 16 = _____	80 – 10 = _____
11.	82 – 47 = _____	96 – 26 = _____
12.	43 – 15 = _____	91 – 28 = _____
13.	40 – 19 = _____	83 – 27 = _____
14.	60 – 39 = _____	71 – 29 = _____
15.	45 – 17 = _____	54 – 19 = _____
16.	32 – 18 = _____	40 – 12 = _____
17.	75 – 68 = _____	50 – 29 = _____
18.	86 – 79 = _____	73 – 59 = _____
19.	82 – 68 = _____	92 – 85 = _____
20.	61 – 33 = _____	42 – 28 = _____

Great Graph Art Around the Year Scholastic Professional Books

The Shadow Knows

1. Make a dot on the graph for each number pair on page 24.
The first one has been done for you.

2. Connect the points in the order that you make them.

3. What picture did you make?_____

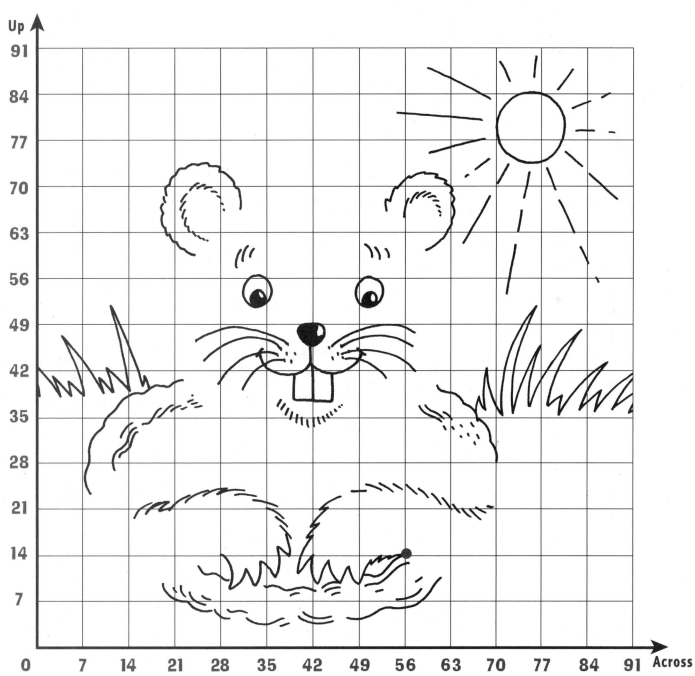

Celebrate School Days!

1. Solve each problem. Example problems have been done for you.

2. Find each number pair on the graph on page 27.

3. Make a dot for each pair. Connect the dots in the order that you make them.

	Across				Up			
1.	2	x	7 = __14__		2	x	11 = __22__	(Example)
2.	2	x	8 = _____		2	x	12 = _____	
3.	2	x	9 = _____		12	x	2 = _____	
4.	2	x	10 = _____		11	x	2 = _____	
5.	10	x	2 = _____		2	x	2 = _____	
6.	9	x	2 = _____		2	x	1 = _____	
7.	8	x	2 = _____		1	x	2 = _____	
8.	7	x	2 = _____		2	x	2 = _____	
9.	2	x	7 = _____		11	x	2 = _____	
10.	2	x	6 = _____		12	x	2 = _____	
11.	5	x	2 = _____		2	x	12 = _____	
12.	2	x	4 = _____		2	x	11 = _____	
13.	4	x	2 = _____		2	x	2 = _____	
14.	2	x	4 = _____		1	x	2 = _____	
15.	1	x	2 = _____		2	x	1 = _____	
16.	2	x	1 = _____		2	x	2 = _____	
17.	2	x	2 = _____		2	x	2 = _____	
18.	2	x	2 = _____		11	x	2 = _____	
19.	1	x	2 = _____		2	x	11 = _____	
20.	2	x	3 = _____		12	x	2 = _____	
21.	3	x	2 = _____		2	x	2 = _____	
22.	4	x	2 = _____		2	x	2 = _____	

Great Graph Art Around the Year Scholastic Professional Books

Celebrate School Days!

1. Make a dot on the graph for each number pair on page 26.
The first one has been done for you.

2. Connect the points in the order that you make them.

3. What picture did you make? _____

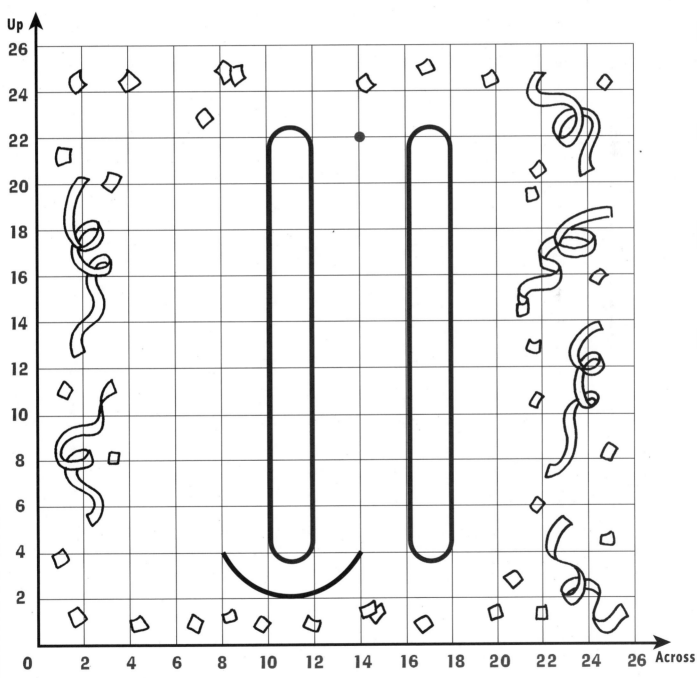

Name _____

Special Delivery

1. Solve each problem. Example problems have been done for you.

2. Find each number pair on the graph on page 29.

3. Make a dot for each pair. Connect the dots in the order that you make them.

	Across			Up		
1.	3 x 12 = __36__			3 x 8 = __24__		(Example)
2.	3 x 11 = _____			3 x 7 = _____		
3.	3 x 10 = _____			3 x 6 = _____		
4.	3 x 9 = _____			3 x 5 = _____		
5.	3 x 8 = _____			5 x 3 = _____		
6.	3 x 7 = _____			3 x 4 = _____		
7.	6 x 3 = _____			3 x 3 = _____		
8.	5 x 3 = _____			3 x 2 = _____		
9.	4 x 3 = _____			3 x 3 = _____		
10.	3 x 3 = _____			4 x 3 = _____		
11.	2 x 3 = _____			5 x 3 = _____		
12.	3 x 2 = _____			7 x 3 = _____		
13.	3 x 3 = _____			3 x 8 = _____		
14.	5 x 3 = _____			3 x 7 = _____		
15.	7 x 3 = _____			8 x 3 = _____		
16.	3 x 8 = _____			7 x 3 = _____		
17.	8 x 3 = _____			5 x 3 = _____		

Great Graph Art Around the Year Scholastic Professional Books

Name _____

Special Delivery

1. Make a dot on the graph for each number pair on page 28.
The first one has been done for you.

2. Connect the points in the order that you make them.

3. What picture did you make? _____

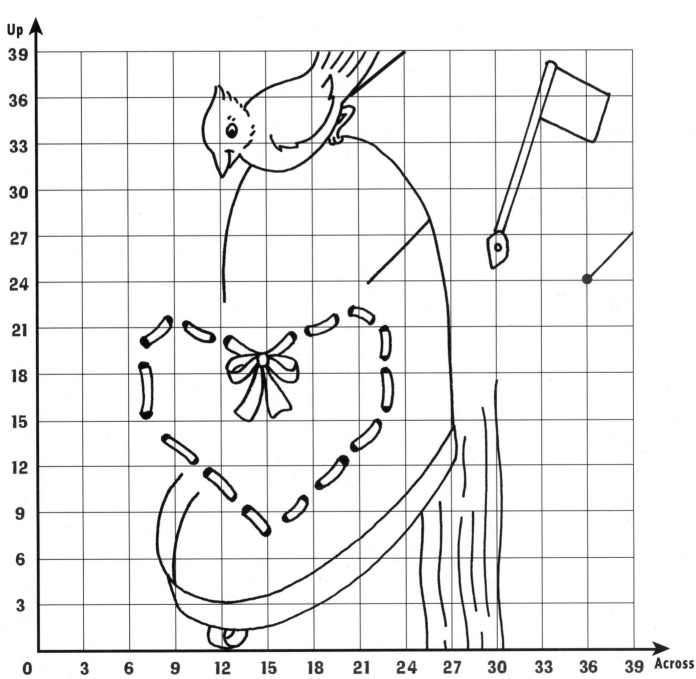

Name _____

Presidents' Day

1. Solve each problem. Example problems have been done for you.

2. Find each number pair on the graph on page 31.

3. Make a dot for each pair. Connect the dots in the order that you make them.

	Across	Up
1.	4 x 3 = __12__	3 x 4 = __12__ (Example)
2.	4 x 1 = _____	4 x 3 = _____
3.	1 x 4 = _____	4 x 2 = _____
4.	4 x 3 = _____	2 x 4 = _____
5.	4 x 10 = _____	4 x 2 = _____
6.	4 x 12 = _____	2 x 4 = _____
7.	12 x 4 = _____	3 x 4 = _____
8.	10 x 4 = _____	4 x 3 = _____
9.	4 x 10 = _____	4 x 6 = _____
10.	10 x 4 = _____	4 x 7 = _____
11.	4 x 10 = _____	4 x 11 = _____
12.	4 x 9 = _____	11 x 4 = _____
13.	4 x 4 = _____	4 x 11 = _____
14.	3 x 4 = _____	11 x 4 = _____
15.	4 x 3 = _____	4 x 8 = _____
16.	3 x 4 = _____	4 x 3 = _____
17.	9 x 4 = _____	3 x 4 = _____
18.	10 x 4 = _____	4 x 3 = _____

Great Graph Art Around the Year Scholastic Professional Books

Presidents' Day

1. Make a dot on the graph for each number pair on page 30.
The first one has been done for you.

2. Connect the points in the order that you make them.

3. What picture did you make?_____

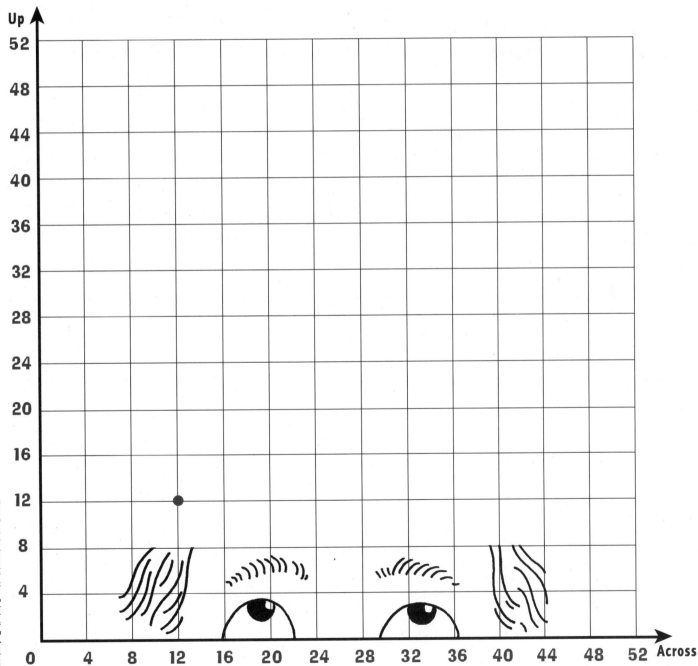

Snow Run

1. Solve each problem. Example problems have been done for you.

2. Find each number pair on the graph on page 33.

3. Make a dot for each pair. Connect the dots in the order that you make them.

	Across				Up			
1.	24	÷	2 =	12	14	÷	2 =	7 (Example)
2.	22	÷	2 =		18	÷	2 =	
3.	20	÷	2 =		22	÷	2 =	
4.	16	÷	2 =		18	÷	2 =	
5.	14	÷	2 =		20	÷	2 =	
6.	12	÷	2 =		18	÷	2 =	
7.	10	÷	2 =		20	÷	2 =	
8.	8	÷	2 =		22	÷	2 =	
9.	6	÷	2 =		24	÷	2 =	
10.	0	÷	2 =		14	÷	2 =	
11.	12	÷	2 =		6	÷	2 =	
12.	18	÷	2 =		2	÷	2 =	
13.	20	÷	2 =		2	÷	2 =	
14.	22	÷	2 =		4	÷	2 =	
15.	22	÷	2 =		6	÷	2 =	
16.	20	÷	2 =		6	÷	2 =	
17.	20	÷	2 =		4	÷	2 =	
18.	16	÷	2 =		6	÷	2 =	
19.	16	÷	2 =		12	÷	2 =	
20.	14	÷	2 =		12	÷	2 =	
21.	12	÷	2 =		8	÷	2 =	
22.	6	÷	2 =		12	÷	2 =	
23.	6	÷	2 =		10	÷	2 =	

Great Graph Art Around the Year Scholastic Professional Books

Snow Run

1. Make a dot on the graph for each number pair on page 32.
The first one has been done for you.

2. Connect the points in the order that you make them.

3. What picture did you make?_____

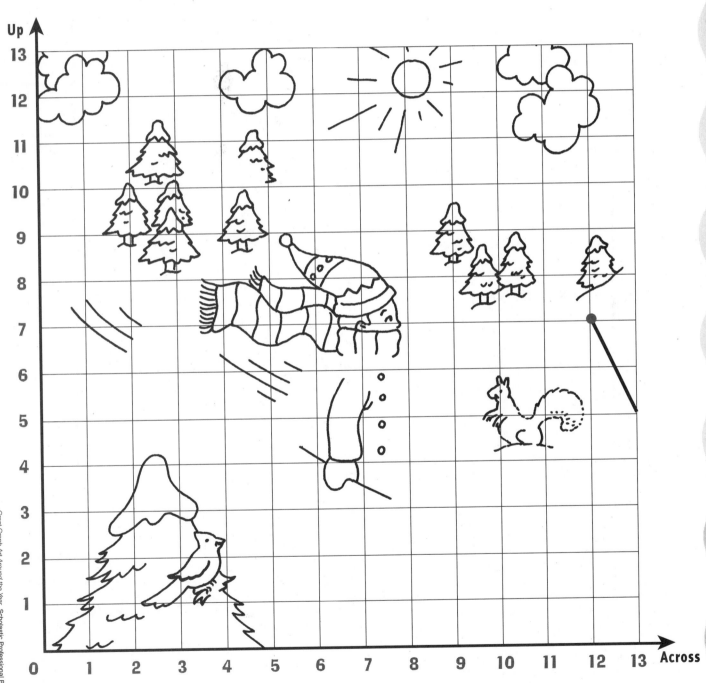

Name _____

Ice Glider

1. Solve each problem. Example problems have been done for you.

2. Find each number pair on the graph on page 35.

3. Make a dot for each pair. Connect the dots in the order that you make them.

	Across	Up
1.	6 ÷ 3 = __2__	12 ÷ 3 = __4__ (Example)
2.	9 ÷ 3 = _____	9 ÷ 3 = _____
3.	15 ÷ 3 = _____	9 ÷ 3 = _____
4.	15 ÷ 3 = _____	12 ÷ 3 = _____
5.	9 ÷ 3 = _____	12 ÷ 3 = _____
6.	9 ÷ 3 = _____	15 ÷ 3 = _____
7.	12 ÷ 3 = _____	18 ÷ 3 = _____
8.	15 ÷ 3 = _____	18 ÷ 3 = _____
9.	21 ÷ 3 = _____	24 ÷ 3 = _____
10.	21 ÷ 3 = _____	33 ÷ 3 = _____
11.	21 ÷ 3 = _____	36 ÷ 3 = _____
12.	30 ÷ 3 = _____	36 ÷ 3 = _____
13.	30 ÷ 3 = _____	33 ÷ 3 = _____
14.	30 ÷ 3 = _____	15 ÷ 3 = _____
15.	27 ÷ 3 = _____	12 ÷ 3 = _____
16.	24 ÷ 3 = _____	12 ÷ 3 = _____
17.	24 ÷ 3 = _____	9 ÷ 3 = _____
18.	33 ÷ 3 = _____	9 ÷ 3 = _____
19.	33 ÷ 3 = _____	12 ÷ 3 = _____

Great Graph Art Around the Year Scholastic Professional Books

Ice Glider

1. Make a dot on the graph for each number pair on page 34.
The first one has been done for you.

2. Connect the points in the order that you make them.

3. What picture did you make? _____

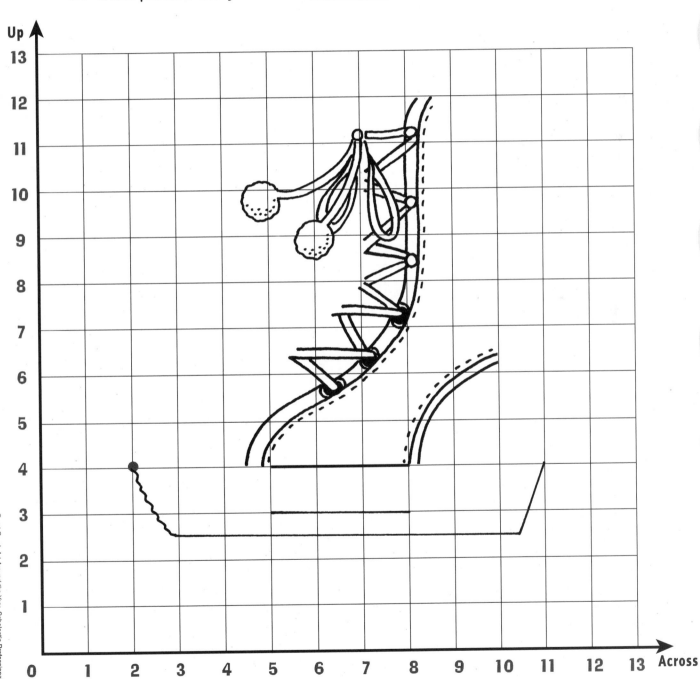

Name _____

Hand Warmer

1. Solve each problem. Example problems have been done for you.

2. Find each number pair on the graph on page 37.

3. Make a dot for each pair. Connect the dots in the order that you make them.

	Across	Up
1.	36 ÷ 4 = ___9___	4 ÷ 4 = ___1___ (Example)
2.	36 ÷ 4 = _____	8 ÷ 4 = _____
3.	36 ÷ 4 = _____	12 ÷ 4 = _____
4.	40 ÷ 4 = _____	16 ÷ 4 = _____
5.	44 ÷ 4 = _____	24 ÷ 4 = _____
6.	48 ÷ 4 = _____	28 ÷ 4 = _____
7.	48 ÷ 4 = _____	32 ÷ 4 = _____
8.	44 ÷ 4 = _____	32 ÷ 4 = _____
9.	40 ÷ 4 = _____	28 ÷ 4 = _____
10.	40 ÷ 4 = _____	36 ÷ 4 = _____
11.	36 ÷ 4 = _____	44 ÷ 4 = _____
12.	28 ÷ 4 = _____	48 ÷ 4 = _____
13.	20 ÷ 4 = _____	48 ÷ 4 = _____
14.	12 ÷ 4 = _____	40 ÷ 4 = _____
15.	12 ÷ 4 = _____	32 ÷ 4 = _____
16.	12 ÷ 4 = _____	24 ÷ 4 = _____
17.	16 ÷ 4 = _____	16 ÷ 4 = _____
18.	16 ÷ 4 = _____	8 ÷ 4 = _____
19.	16 ÷ 4 = _____	4 ÷ 4 = _____
20.	36 ÷ 4 = _____	4 ÷ 4 = _____

Great Graph Art Around the Year Scholastic Professional Books

Name _____

Hand Warmer

1. Make a dot on the graph for each number pair on page 36.
   The first one has been done for you.

2. Connect the points in the order that you make them.

3. What picture did you make? _____

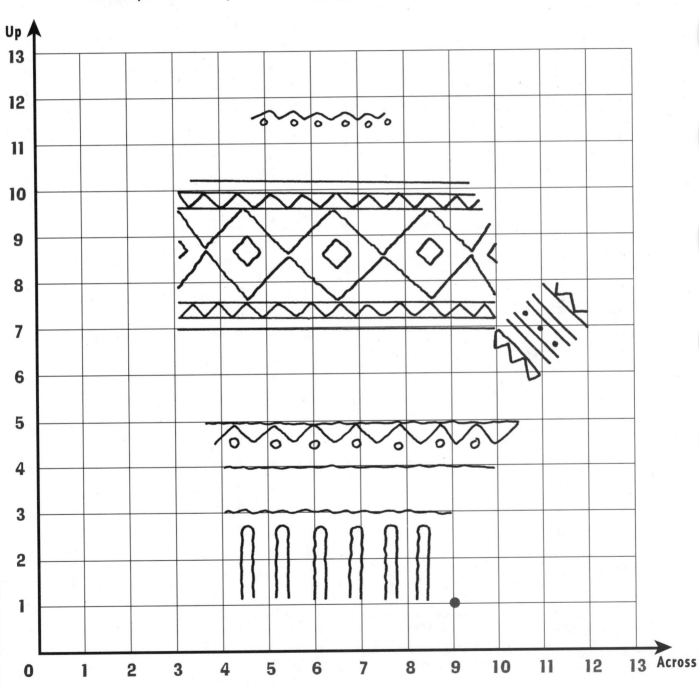

Name _____

Lucky Charm

1. Solve each problem. Example problems have been done for you.

2. Find each number pair on the graph on page 39.

3. Make a dot for each pair. Connect the dots in the order that you make them.

	Across				Up			
1.	5	x	5 = __25__		5	x	3 = __15__	(Example)
2.	5	x	6 = _____		5	x	4 = _____	
3.	5	x	7 = _____		3	x	5 = _____	
4.	5	x	8 = _____		5	x	3 = _____	
5.	5	x	9 = _____		4	x	5 = _____	
6.	8	x	5 = _____		5	x	5 = _____	
7.	9	x	5 = _____		5	x	6 = _____	
8.	5	x	9 = _____		7	x	5 = _____	
9.	5	x	7 = _____		6	x	5 = _____	
10.	6	x	5 = _____		5	x	6 = _____	
11.	5	x	5 = _____		6	x	5 = _____	
12.	3	x	5 = _____		5	x	7 = _____	
13.	5	x	3 = _____		6	x	5 = _____	
14.	4	x	5 = _____		5	x	5 = _____	
15.	5	x	3 = _____		5	x	4 = _____	
16.	5	x	4 = _____		3	x	5 = _____	
17.	5	x	3 = _____		5	x	1 = _____	
18.	5	x	5 = _____		1	x	5 = _____	
19.	6	x	5 = _____		5	x	2 = _____	
20.	7	x	5 = _____		5	x	1 = _____	
21.	5	x	9 = _____		1	x	5 = _____	
22.	8	x	5 = _____		5	x	3 = _____	
23.	5	x	7 = _____		4	x	5 = _____	
24.	6	x	5 = _____		5	x	6 = _____	
25.	5	x	5 = _____		5	x	4 = _____	
26.	4	x	5 = _____		5	x	3 = _____	
27.	5	x	5 = _____		3	x	5 = _____	

⭐ **Here's More!**

Now add something extra special to your picture!

	Across			Up		
1.	5	x 9 = ____		3	x 5 = ____	
2.	5	x 10 = ____		5	x 3 = ____	
3.	5	x 11 = ____		3	x 5 = ____	
4.	5	x 12 = ____		5	x 3 = ____	

Great Graph Art Around the Year Scholastic Professional Books

Lucky Charm

1. Make a dot on the graph for each number pair on page 38.
The first one has been done for you.

2. Connect the points in the order that you make them.

3. What picture did you make?_____

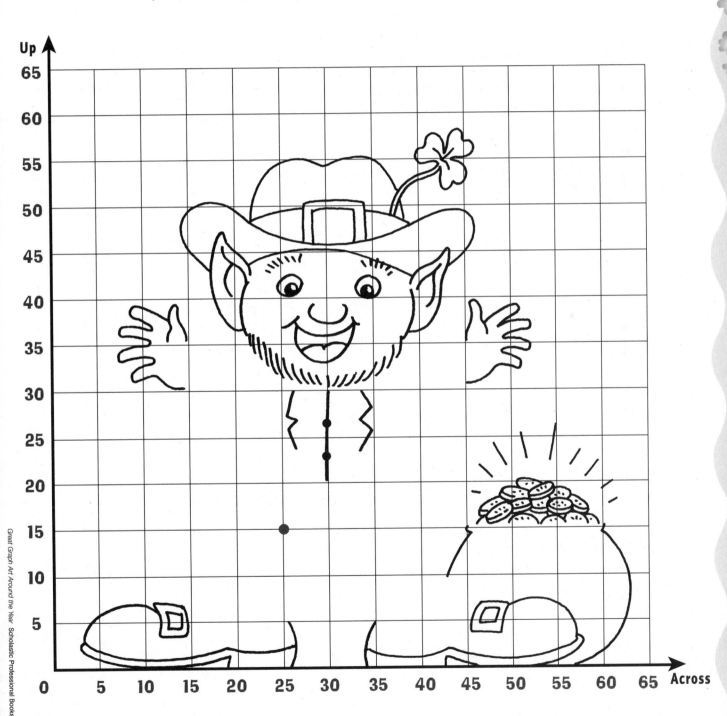

Name _____

Soar Into Spring!

1. Solve each problem. Example problems have been done for you.

2. Find each number pair on the graph on page 41.

3. Make a dot for each pair. Connect the dots in the order that you make them.

	Across	Up
1.	6 x 5 = __30__	6 x 3 = __18__ (Example)
2.	5 x 6 = _____	6 x 1 = _____
3.	6 x 8 = _____	1 x 6 = _____
4.	8 x 6 = _____	3 x 6 = _____
5.	6 x 9 = _____	6 x 4 = _____
6.	11 x 6 = _____	6 x 6 = _____
7.	6 x 11 = _____	6 x 7 = _____
8.	11 x 6 = _____	6 x 10 = _____
9.	10 x 6 = _____	6 x 11 = _____
10.	6 x 8 = _____	6 x 12 = _____
11.	5 x 6 = _____	12 x 6 = _____
12.	6 x 3 = _____	11 x 6 = _____
13.	6 x 2 = _____	10 x 6 = _____
14.	2 x 6 = _____	7 x 6 = _____
15.	6 x 2 = _____	6 x 6 = _____
16.	6 x 4 = _____	4 x 6 = _____
17.	6 x 5 = _____	6 x 3 = _____

Great Graph Art Around the Year Scholastic Professional Books

Soar Into Spring!

1. Make a dot on the graph for each number pair on page 40.
The first one has been done for you.

2. Connect the points in the order that you make them.

3. What picture did you make?_____

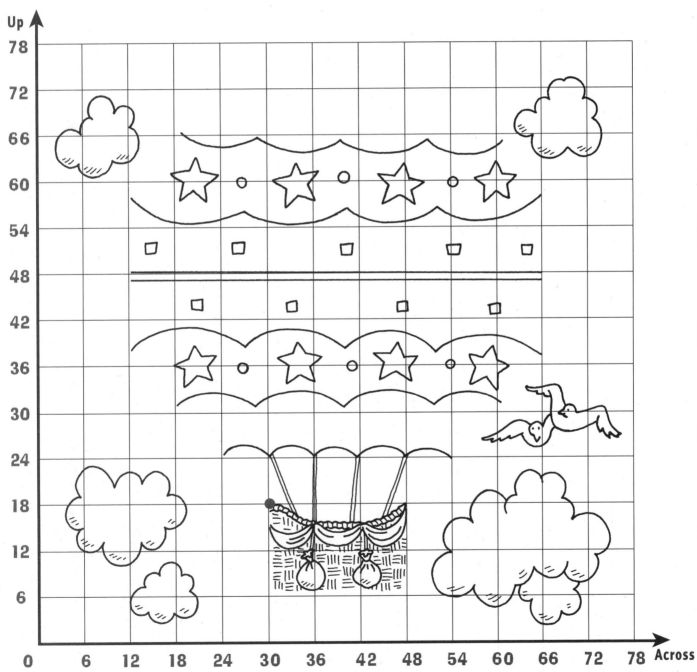

Name _____

Carrot Cruncher

1. Solve each problem. Example problems have been done for you.

2. Find each number pair on the graph on page 43.

3. Make a dot for each pair. Connect the dots in the order that you make them.

	Across	Up
1.	7 x 9 = __63__	7 x 0 = __0__ (Example)
2.	7 x 11 = _____	2 x 7 = _____
3.	11 x 7 = _____	4 x 7 = _____
4.	7 x 10 = _____	6 x 7 = _____
5.	9 x 7 = _____	7 x 9 = _____
6.	10 x 7 = _____	7 x 11 = _____
7.	11 x 7 = _____	9 x 7 = _____
8.	7 x 12 = _____	10 x 7 = _____
9.	7 x 10 = _____	12 x 7 = _____
10.	8 x 7 = _____	9 x 7 = _____
11.	7 x 8 = _____	6 x 7 = _____
12.	7 x 5 = _____	7 x 6 = _____
13.	5 x 7 = _____	7 x 7 = _____
14.	7 x 5 = _____	7 x 11 = _____
15.	3 x 7 = _____	12 x 7 = _____
16.	1 x 7 = _____	10 x 7 = _____
17.	7 x 1 = _____	9 x 7 = _____
18.	7 x 3 = _____	11 x 7 = _____
19.	4 x 7 = _____	7 x 10 = _____
20.	3 x 7 = _____	7 x 6 = _____
21.	2 x 7 = _____	4 x 7 = _____
22.	7 x 2 = _____	2 x 7 = _____
23.	7 x 4 = _____	0 x 7 = _____

Great Graph Art Around the Year Scholastic Professional Books

Carrot Cruncher

1. Make a dot on the graph for each number pair on page 42.
   The first one has been done for you.

2. Connect the points in the order that you make them.

3. What picture did you make?_____

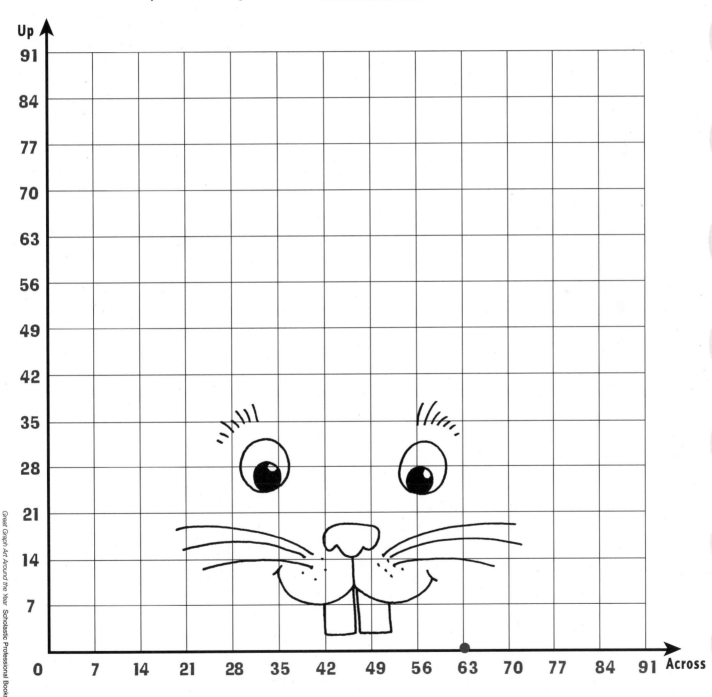

Name _____

Creepy Crawly

1. Solve each problem. Example problems have been done for you.

2. Find each number pair on the graph on page 45.

3. Make a dot for each pair. Connect the dots in the order that you make them.

	Across				Up			
1.	6	x	8 = __48__		8	x	10 = __80__	(Example)
2.	4	x	8 = _____		8	x	9 = _____	
3.	3	x	8 = _____		8	x	8 = _____	
4.	8	x	3 = _____		5	x	8 = _____	
5.	8	x	4 = _____		4	x	8 = _____	
6.	8	x	5 = _____		3	x	8 = _____	
7.	6	x	8 = _____		8	x	3 = _____	
8.	7	x	8 = _____		8	x	10 = _____	
9.	8	x	8 = _____		3	x	8 = _____	
10.	9	x	8 = _____		8	x	3 = _____	
11.	8	x	11 = _____		5	x	8 = _____	
12.	11	x	8 = _____		8	x	8 = _____	
13.	10	x	8 = _____		9	x	8 = _____	
14.	8	x	8 = _____		10	x	8 = _____	

⭐ **Here's More!** Now give your creepy crawly a home!

	Across				Up		
1.	8	x	11 = _____		8	x	10 = _____
2.	8	x	12 = _____		8	x	9 = _____
3.	12	x	8 = _____		8	x	5 = _____
4.	9	x	8 = _____		8	x	2 = _____
5.	3	x	8 = _____		1	x	8 = _____
6.	8	x	2 = _____		5	x	8 = _____
7.	3	x	8 = _____		8	x	9 = _____
8.	5	x	8 = _____		8	x	11 = _____
9.	8	x	8 = _____		12	x	8 = _____
10.	10	x	8 = _____		11	x	8 = _____
11.	8	x	10 = _____		10	x	8 = _____
12.	8	x	11 = _____		8	x	10 = _____

Great Graph Art Around the Year Scholastic Professional Books

Creepy Crawly

1. Make a dot on the graph for each number pair on page 44.
The first one has been done for you.

2. Connect the points in the order that you make them.

3. What picture did you make?_____

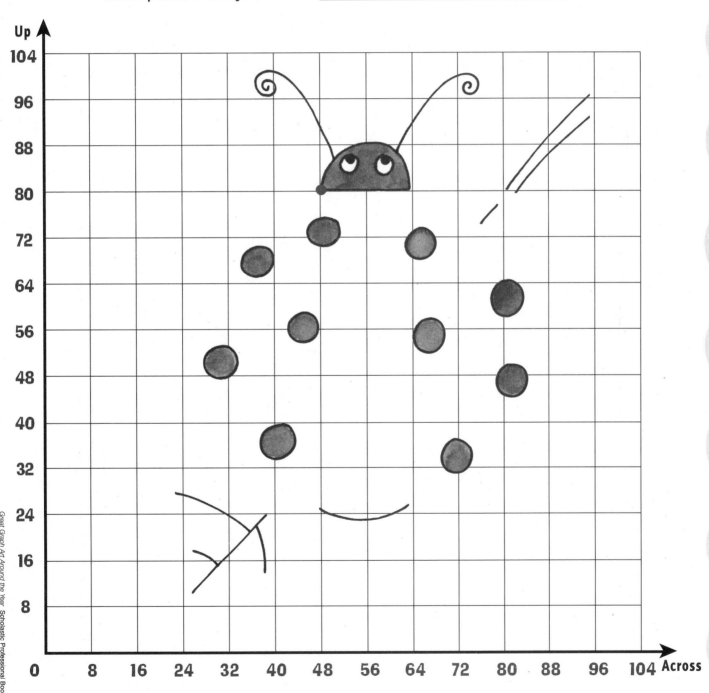

Name _____

Whee!

1. Solve each problem. Example problems have been done for you.

2. Find each number pair on the graph on page 47.

3. Make a dot for each pair. Connect the dots in the order that you make them.

	Across	Up
1.	1 x 9 = __9__	9 x 12 = __108__ (Example)
2.	9 x 1 = _____	9 x 11 = _____
3.	9 x 2 = _____	9 x 10 = _____
4.	3 x 9 = _____	9 x 9 = _____
5.	4 x 9 = _____	9 x 8 = _____
6.	9 x 5 = _____	9 x 7 = _____
7.	9 x 6 = _____	6 x 9 = _____
8.	7 x 9 = _____	5 x 9 = _____
9.	9 x 8 = _____	9 x 4 = _____
10.	9 x 9 = _____	3 x 9 = _____
11.	11 x 9 = _____	9 x 3 = _____
12.	9 x 9 = _____	4 x 9 = _____
13.	8 x 9 = _____	9 x 5 = _____
14.	7 x 9 = _____	6 x 9 = _____
15.	9 x 6 = _____	9 x 7 = _____
16.	5 x 9 = _____	8 x 9 = _____
17.	4 x 9 = _____	9 x 9 = _____
18.	9 x 3 = _____	10 x 9 = _____
19.	2 x 9 = _____	11 x 9 = _____
20.	9 x 1 = _____	9 x 11 = _____

Great Graph Art Around the Year Scholastic Professional Books

Name _____

Multiplication x9

Whee!

1. Make a dot on the graph for each number pair on page 46.
The first one has been done for you.

2. Connect the points in the order that you make them.

3. What picture did you make? _____

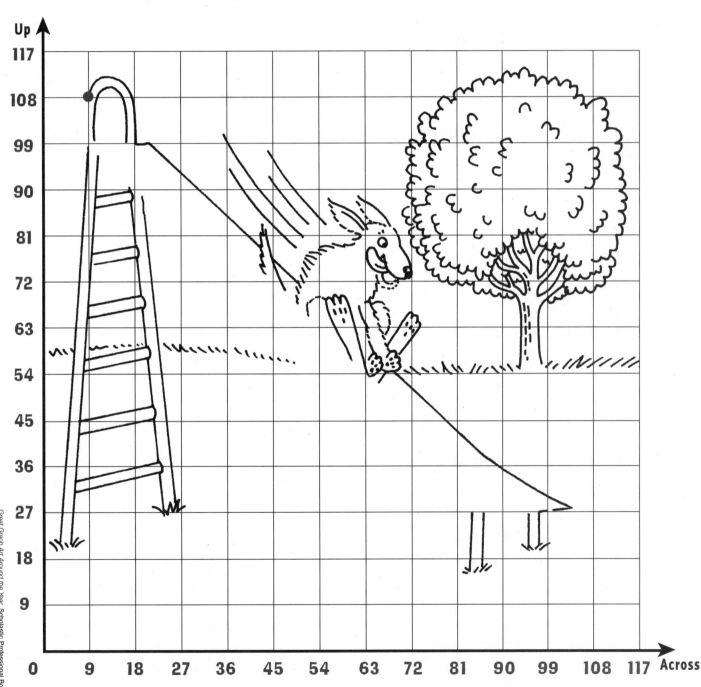

Multiplication x10

Name _____

Kick It!

1. Solve each problem. Example problems have been done for you.

2. Find each number pair on the graph on page 49.

3. Make a dot for each pair. Connect the dots in the order that you make them.

	Across	Up
1.	2 x 10 = __20__	7 x 10 = __70__ (Example)
2.	10 x 2 = _____	8 x 10 = _____
3.	10 x 3 = _____	10 x 10 = _____
4.	5 x 10 = _____	10 x 11 = _____
5.	10 x 8 = _____	11 x 10 = _____
6.	10 x 10 = _____	10 x 10 = _____
7.	11 x 10 = _____	8 x 10 = _____
8.	10 x 11 = _____	6 x 10 = _____
9.	10 x 10 = _____	4 x 10 = _____
10.	10 x 8 = _____	10 x 3 = _____
11.	5 x 10 = _____	3 x 10 = _____
12.	10 x 3 = _____	10 x 4 = _____
13.	2 x 10 = _____	6 x 10 = _____
14.	10 x 2 = _____	7 x 10 = _____
15.	4 x 10 = _____	10 x 7 = _____
16.	5 x 10 = _____	10 x 5 = _____
17.	8 x 10 = _____	5 x 10 = _____
18.	10 x 9 = _____	10 x 7 = _____
19.	8 x 10 = _____	9 x 10 = _____
20.	5 x 10 = _____	10 x 9 = _____
21.	4 x 10 = _____	7 x 10 = _____

Great Graph Art Around the Year Scholastic Professional Books

48

Kick It!

1. Make a dot on the graph for each number pair on page 48.
The first one has been done for you.

2. Connect the points in the order that you make them.

3. What picture did you make?_____

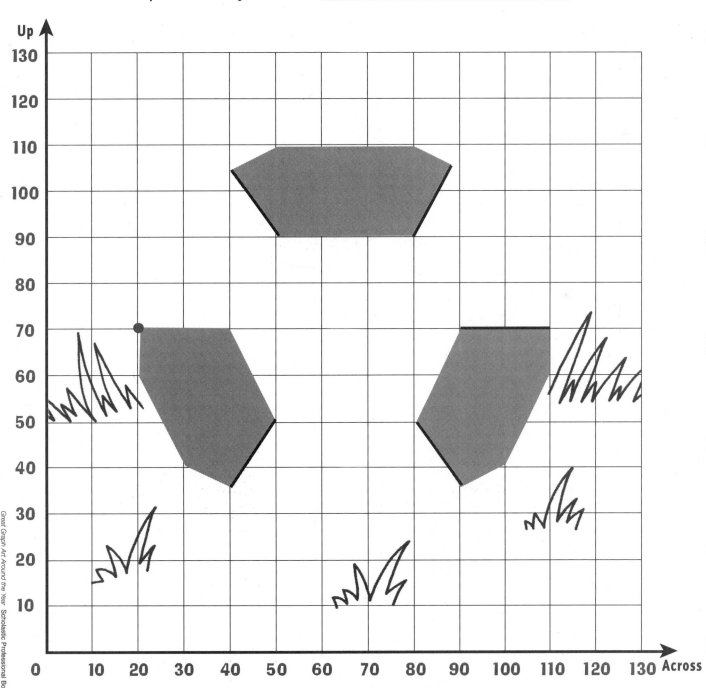

Name _____

April Showers

1. Solve each problem. Example problems have been done for you.

2. Find each number pair on the graph on page 51.

3. Make a dot for each pair. Connect the dots in the order that you make them.

	Across				Up			
1.	35	÷	5 =	7	40	÷	5 =	8 (Example)
2.	45	÷	5 =		30	÷	5 =	
3.	45	÷	5 =		35	÷	5 =	
4.	50	÷	5 =		35	÷	5 =	
5.	50	÷	5 =		30	÷	5 =	
6.	45	÷	5 =		25	÷	5 =	
7.	40	÷	5 =		30	÷	5 =	
8.	45	÷	5 =		15	÷	5 =	
9.	40	÷	5 =		15	÷	5 =	
10.	40	÷	5 =		10	÷	5 =	
11.	45	÷	5 =		5	÷	5 =	
12.	35	÷	5 =		5	÷	5 =	
13.	35	÷	5 =		15	÷	5 =	
14.	30	÷	5 =		15	÷	5 =	
15.	30	÷	5 =		5	÷	5 =	
16.	20	÷	5 =		5	÷	5 =	
17.	25	÷	5 =		10	÷	5 =	
18.	25	÷	5 =		15	÷	5 =	
19.	20	÷	5 =		15	÷	5 =	
20.	25	÷	5 =		30	÷	5 =	
21.	20	÷	5 =		25	÷	5 =	
22.	15	÷	5 =		25	÷	5 =	
23.	30	÷	5 =		40	÷	5 =	

⭐ **Here's More!** Now add a surprise for the bird in your picture!

	Across	Up
1.	50 ÷ 5 =	5 ÷ 5 =
2.	50 ÷ 5 =	15 ÷ 5 =
3.	45 ÷ 5 =	20 ÷ 5 =
4.	60 ÷ 5 =	20 ÷ 5 =
5.	55 ÷ 5 =	15 ÷ 5 =
6.	55 ÷ 5 =	5 ÷ 5 =

Division
÷5

April Showers

1. Make a dot on the graph for each number pair on page 50. The first one has been done for you.

2. Connect the points in the order that you make them.

3. What picture did you make?_____

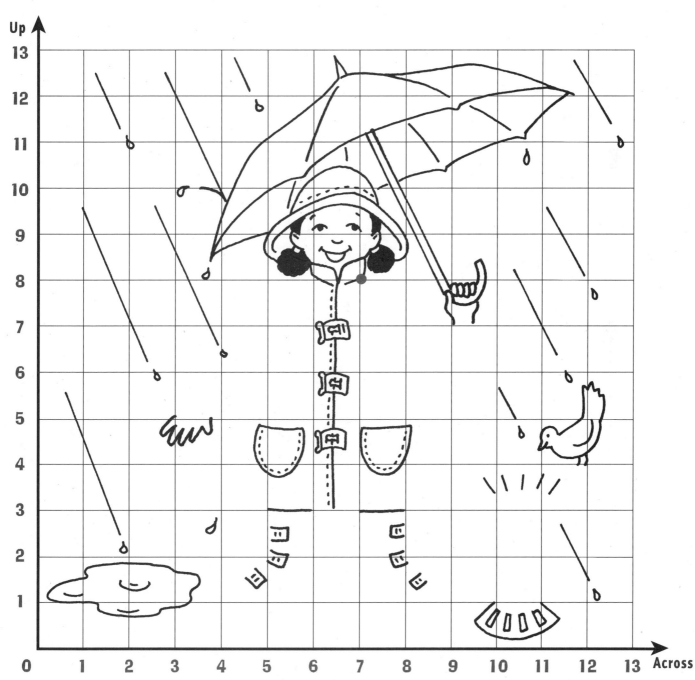

Name _____

May Day

1. Solve each problem. Example problems have been done for you.

2. Find each number pair on the graph on page 53.

3. Make a dot for each pair. Connect the dots in the order that you make them.

	Across	Up
1.	6 ÷ 6 = __1__	36 ÷ 6 = __6__ (Example)
2.	66 ÷ 6 = _____	36 ÷ 6 = _____
3.	72 ÷ 6 = _____	42 ÷ 6 = _____
4.	66 ÷ 6 = _____	24 ÷ 6 = _____
5.	54 ÷ 6 = _____	12 ÷ 6 = _____
6.	24 ÷ 6 = _____	12 ÷ 6 = _____
7.	12 ÷ 6 = _____	24 ÷ 6 = _____
8.	6 ÷ 6 = _____	36 ÷ 6 = _____
9.	18 ÷ 6 = _____	42 ÷ 6 = _____
10.	30 ÷ 6 = _____	42 ÷ 6 = _____
11.	30 ÷ 6 = _____	60 ÷ 6 = _____
12.	36 ÷ 6 = _____	66 ÷ 6 = _____
13.	42 ÷ 6 = _____	66 ÷ 6 = _____
14.	48 ÷ 6 = _____	60 ÷ 6 = _____
15.	48 ÷ 6 = _____	42 ÷ 6 = _____

Great Graph Art Around the Year Scholastic Professional Books

May Day

1. Make a dot on the graph for each number pair on page 52.
The first one has been done for you.

2. Connect the points in the order that you make them.

3. What picture did you make?_____

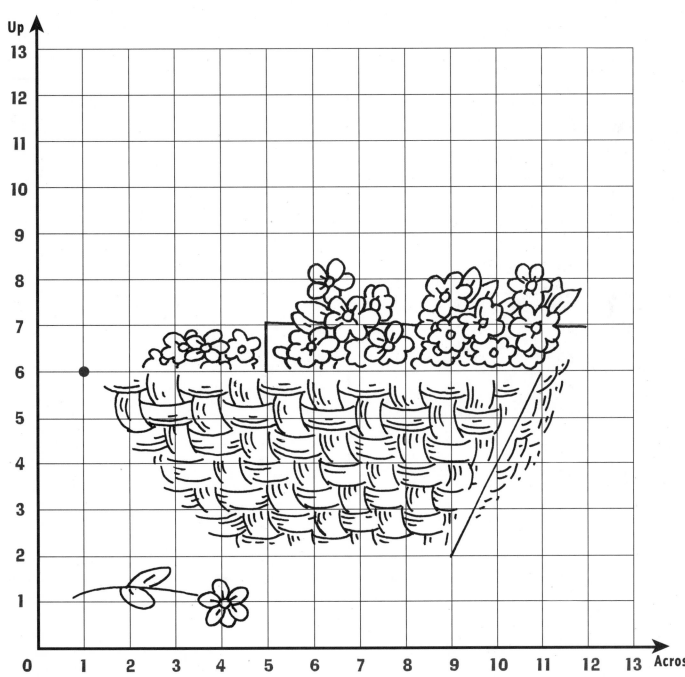

Name _____

Fiesta!

1. Solve each problem. Example problems have been done for you.

2. Find each number pair on the graph on page 55.

3. Make a dot for each pair. Connect the dots in the order that you make them.

	Across	Up
1.	49 ÷ 7 = __7__	84 ÷ 7 = __12__ (Example)
2.	49 ÷ 7 = _____	70 ÷ 7 = _____
3.	35 ÷ 7 = _____	70 ÷ 7 = _____
4.	28 ÷ 7 = _____	77 ÷ 7 = _____
5.	21 ÷ 7 = _____	77 ÷ 7 = _____
6.	7 ÷ 7 = _____	63 ÷ 7 = _____
7.	7 ÷ 7 = _____	56 ÷ 7 = _____
8.	14 ÷ 7 = _____	56 ÷ 7 = _____
9.	21 ÷ 7 = _____	63 ÷ 7 = _____
10.	28 ÷ 7 = _____	56 ÷ 7 = _____
11.	35 ÷ 7 = _____	49 ÷ 7 = _____
12.	42 ÷ 7 = _____	49 ÷ 7 = _____
13.	56 ÷ 7 = _____	49 ÷ 7 = _____
14.	63 ÷ 7 = _____	49 ÷ 7 = _____
15.	70 ÷ 7 = _____	56 ÷ 7 = _____
16.	70 ÷ 7 = _____	63 ÷ 7 = _____
17.	63 ÷ 7 = _____	70 ÷ 7 = _____
18.	49 ÷ 7 = _____	70 ÷ 7 = _____

Great Graph Art Around the Year Scholastic Professional Books

Name _____

Fiesta!

1. Make a dot on the graph for each number pair on page 54.
The first one has been done for you.

2. Connect the points in the order that you make them.

3. What picture did you make? _____

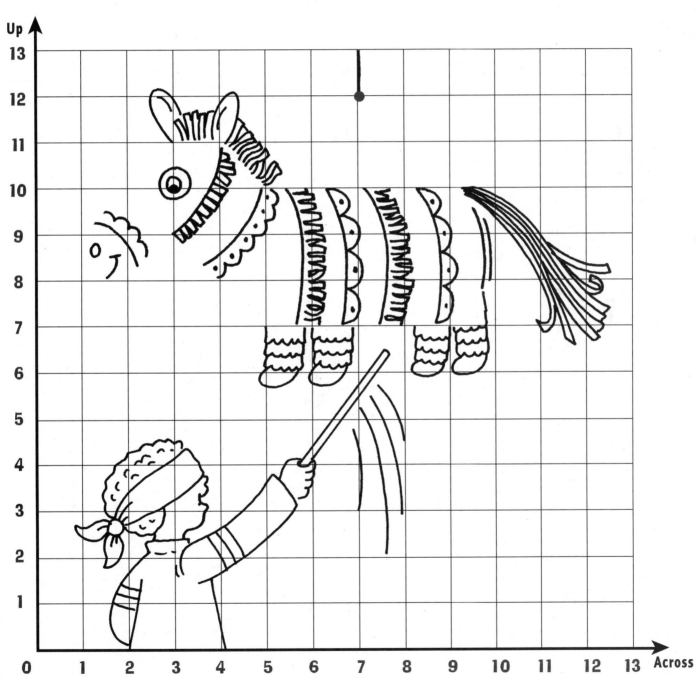

Seashore Fun

1. Solve each problem. Example problems have been done for you.

2. Find each number pair on the graph on page 57.

3. Make a dot for each pair. Connect the dots in the order that you make them.

	Across	Up
1.	48 ÷ 8 = __6__	96 ÷ 8 = __12__ (Example)
2.	32 ÷ 8 = _____	72 ÷ 8 = _____
3.	32 ÷ 8 = _____	88 ÷ 8 = _____
4.	24 ÷ 8 = _____	88 ÷ 8 = _____
5.	24 ÷ 8 = _____	80 ÷ 8 = _____
6.	16 ÷ 8 = _____	80 ÷ 8 = _____
7.	16 ÷ 8 = _____	88 ÷ 8 = _____
8.	8 ÷ 8 = _____	88 ÷ 8 = _____
9.	8 ÷ 8 = _____	24 ÷ 8 = _____
10.	32 ÷ 8 = _____	24 ÷ 8 = _____
11.	40 ÷ 8 = _____	24 ÷ 8 = _____
12.	48 ÷ 8 = _____	8 ÷ 8 = _____
13.	64 ÷ 8 = _____	8 ÷ 8 = _____
14.	56 ÷ 8 = _____	24 ÷ 8 = _____
15.	64 ÷ 8 = _____	24 ÷ 8 = _____
16.	88 ÷ 8 = _____	24 ÷ 8 = _____
17.	88 ÷ 8 = _____	88 ÷ 8 = _____
18.	80 ÷ 8 = _____	88 ÷ 8 = _____
19.	80 ÷ 8 = _____	80 ÷ 8 = _____
20.	72 ÷ 8 = _____	80 ÷ 8 = _____
21.	72 ÷ 8 = _____	88 ÷ 8 = _____
22.	64 ÷ 8 = _____	88 ÷ 8 = _____
23.	64 ÷ 8 = _____	72 ÷ 8 = _____
24.	48 ÷ 8 = _____	96 ÷ 8 = _____

Great Graph Art Around the Year   Scholastic Professional Books

Seashore Fun

1. Make a dot on the graph for each number pair on page 56.
   The first one has been done for you.

2. Connect the points in the order that you make them.

3. What picture did you make? _____

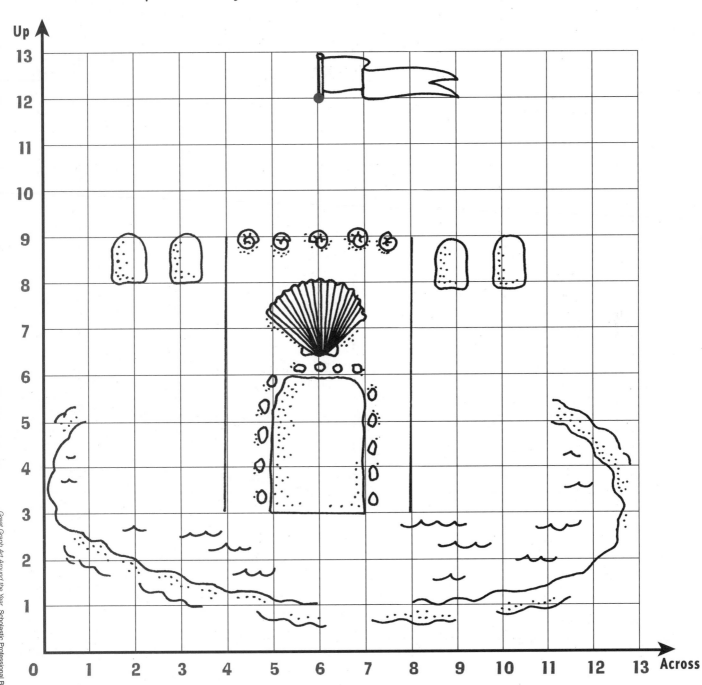

Great Graph Art Around the Year Scholastic Professional Books

Name _____

Summer Storm

1. Solve each problem. Example problems have been done for you.

2. Find each number pair on the graph on page 59.

3. Make a dot for each pair. Connect the dots in the order that you make them.

	Across	Up
1.	81 ÷ 9 = __9__	108 ÷ 9 = __12__ (Example)
2.	54 ÷ 9 = _____	90 ÷ 9 = _____
3.	36 ÷ 9 = _____	81 ÷ 9 = _____
4.	63 ÷ 9 = _____	63 ÷ 9 = _____
5.	45 ÷ 9 = _____	45 ÷ 9 = _____
6.	63 ÷ 9 = _____	36 ÷ 9 = _____
7.	18 ÷ 9 = _____	18 ÷ 9 = _____
8.	63 ÷ 9 = _____	9 ÷ 9 = _____
9.	36 ÷ 9 = _____	18 ÷ 9 = _____
10.	72 ÷ 9 = _____	36 ÷ 9 = _____
11.	54 ÷ 9 = _____	45 ÷ 9 = _____
12.	72 ÷ 9 = _____	63 ÷ 9 = _____
13.	63 ÷ 9 = _____	72 ÷ 9 = _____
14.	54 ÷ 9 = _____	81 ÷ 9 = _____
15.	81 ÷ 9 = _____	108 ÷ 9 = _____

Great Graph Art Around the Year Scholastic Professional Books

Summer Storm

1. Make a dot on the graph for each number pair on page 58.
The first one has been done for you.

2. Connect the points in the order that you make them.

3. What picture did you make?_____

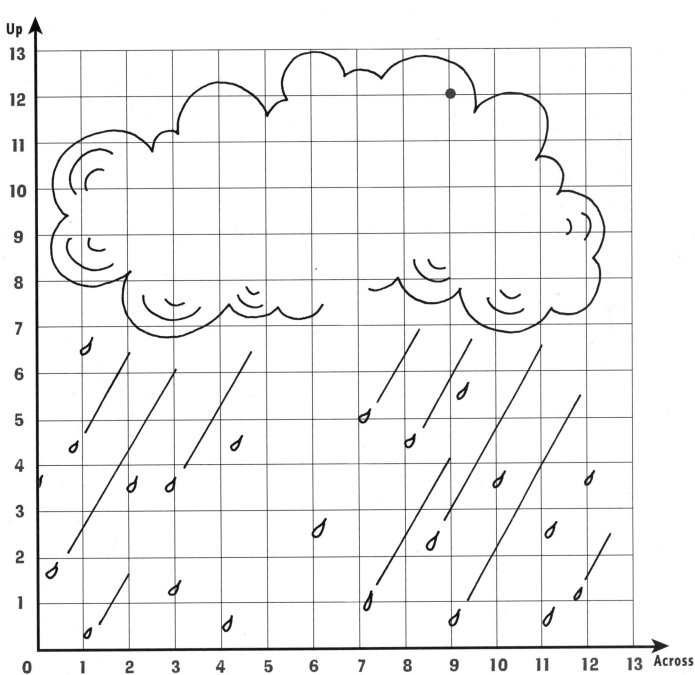

Icy Treat

1. Solve each problem. Example problems have been done for you.

2. Find each number pair on the graph on page 61.

3. Make a dot for each pair. Connect the dots in the order that you make them.

	Across	Up
1.	40 ÷ 10 = __4__	110 ÷ 10 = __11__ (Example)
2.	40 ÷ 10 = _____	100 ÷ 10 = _____
3.	40 ÷ 10 = _____	80 ÷ 10 = _____
4.	40 ÷ 10 = _____	40 ÷ 10 = _____
5.	50 ÷ 10 = _____	40 ÷ 10 = _____
6.	50 ÷ 10 = _____	30 ÷ 10 = _____
7.	50 ÷ 10 = _____	10 ÷ 10 = _____
8.	60 ÷ 10 = _____	10 ÷ 10 = _____
9.	60 ÷ 10 = _____	40 ÷ 10 = _____
10.	70 ÷ 10 = _____	40 ÷ 10 = _____
11.	70 ÷ 10 = _____	10 ÷ 10 = _____
12.	80 ÷ 10 = _____	10 ÷ 10 = _____
13.	80 ÷ 10 = _____	20 ÷ 10 = _____
14.	80 ÷ 10 = _____	40 ÷ 10 = _____
15.	90 ÷ 10 = _____	40 ÷ 10 = _____
16.	90 ÷ 10 = _____	90 ÷ 10 = _____
17.	90 ÷ 10 = _____	110 ÷ 10 = _____

Great Graph Art Around the Year Scholastic Professional Books

Icy Treat

1. Make a dot on the graph for each number pair on page 60.
The first one has been done for you.

2. Connect the points in the order that you make them.

3. What picture did you make? _____

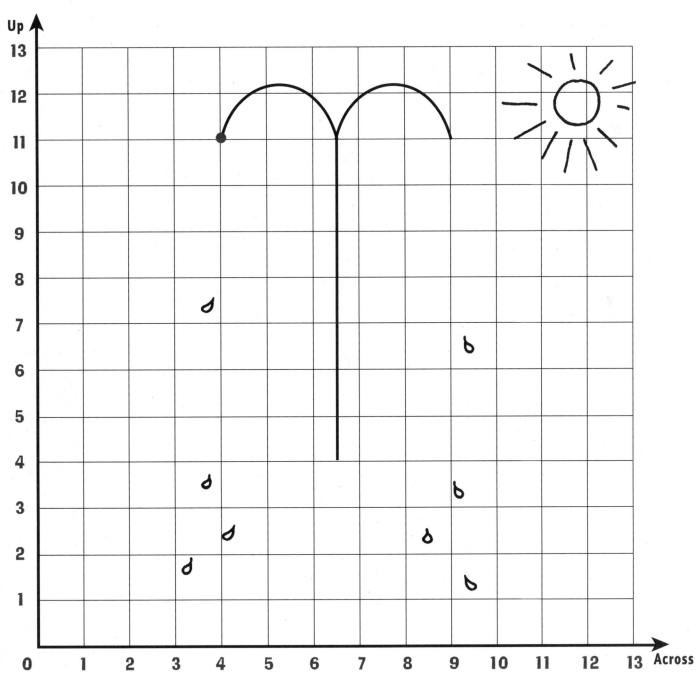

Name _____

Vacation Time!

1. Solve each problem. Example problems have been done for you.

2. Find each number pair on the graph on page 63.

3. Make a dot for each pair. Connect the dots in the order that you make them.

	Across	Up
1.	24 − 24 = __0__	1 + 10 = __11__ (Example)
2.	24 ÷ 12 = _____	4 + 9 = _____
3.	95 − 92 = _____	1 x 11 = _____
4.	4 x 1 = _____	3 + 9 = _____
5.	25 ÷ 5 = _____	66 ÷ 6 = _____
6.	35 − 29 = _____	8 + 3 = _____
7.	45 ÷ 9 = _____	37 − 29 = _____
8.	28 ÷ 7 = _____	2 x 3 = _____
9.	22 − 19 = _____	1 + 3 = _____
10.	18 ÷ 9 = _____	89 − 87 = _____
11.	1 x 1 = _____	55 − 55 = _____
12.	54 ÷ 9 = _____	10 x 0 = _____
13.	78 − 67 = _____	0 ÷ 0 = _____
14.	50 ÷ 5 = _____	46 − 44 = _____
15.	3 x 3 = _____	1 x 4 = _____
16.	24 ÷ 3 = _____	33 − 27 = _____
17.	4 + 3 = _____	4 x 2 = _____
18.	1 + 5 = _____	4 + 7 = _____
19.	19 − 11 = _____	26 − 15 = _____
20.	3 x 3 = _____	8 + 5 = _____
21.	11 x 1 = _____	77 ÷ 7 = _____
22.	6 + 7 = _____	6 x 2 = _____

Great Graph Art Around the Year Scholastic Professional Books

Vacation Time!

1. Make a dot on the graph for each number pair on page 62.
The first one has been done for you.

2. Connect the points in the order that you make them.

3. What picture did you make? _____

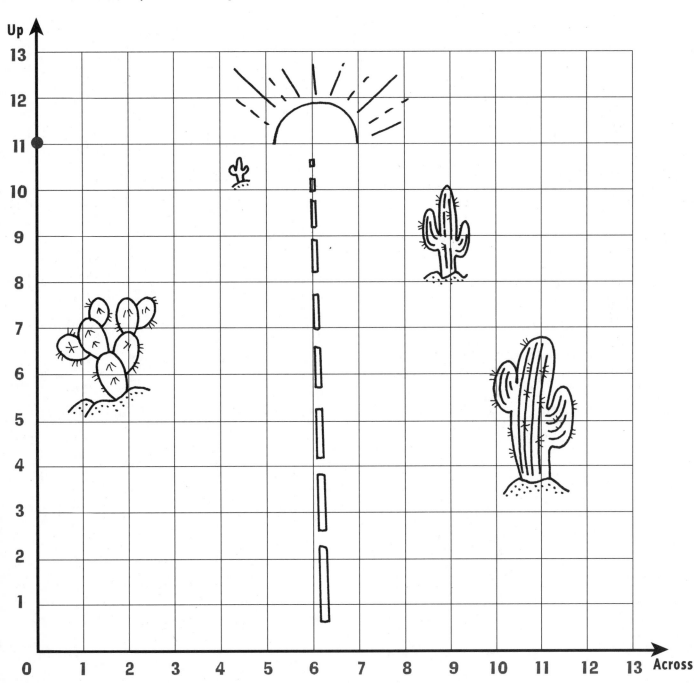

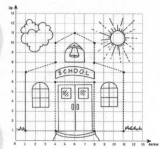

Answer Key

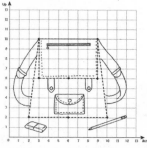

Page 6
So Long, Summer!

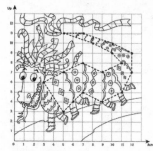

Page 23
Happy New Year!

Page 7
Bag for Books

Page 10
Harvest Time

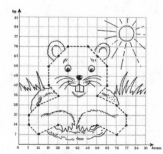

Page 15
Sweet Treat

Page 8
Fun in the Orchard

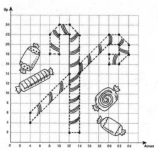

Page 11
All Aboard!

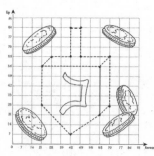

Page 17
Hanukkah Fun

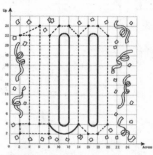

Page 25
The Shadow Knows

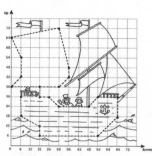

Page 12
Gobble! Gobble!

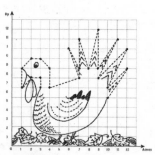

Page 19
Kwanzaa Time

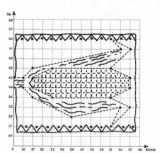

Page 27
Celebrate School Days!

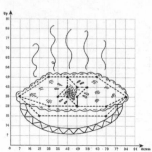

Page 9
Trick-or-Treat!

Page 13
Holiday Dessert

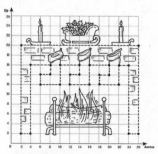

Page 21
Warm and Cozy

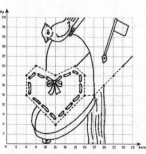

Page 29
Special Delivery

64